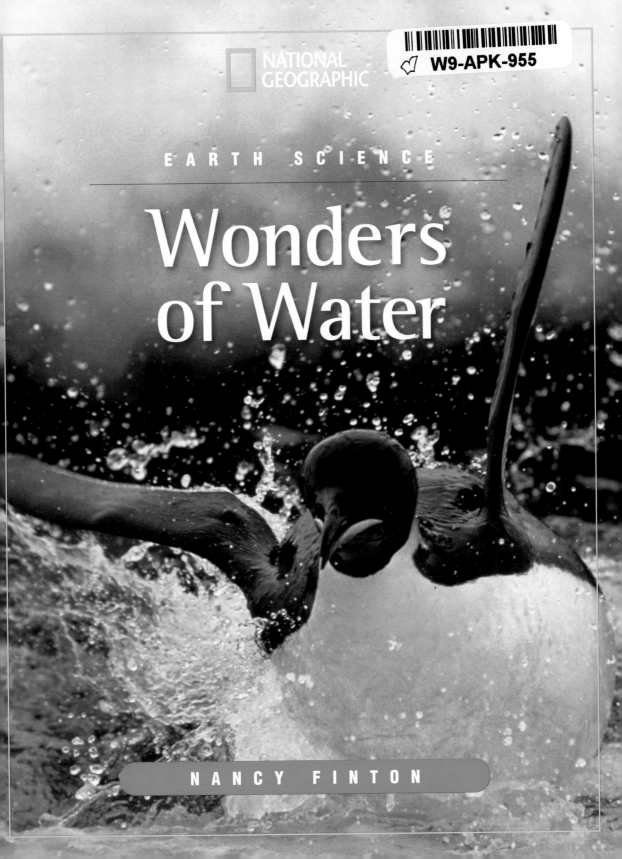

NATIONAL GEOGRAPHIC

EARTH SCIENCE

Wonders of Water

NANCY FINTON

PICTURE CREDITS
Cover: © Digital Stock; Page 1 © Johnny Johnson/Alaska Stock;
pages 2-3 © Wes Skiles/National Geographic Image Collection; page 4
© Raul Martin; pages 4-5 © Tony Freeman/PhotoEdit, page 5 © Hemera
Technologies Inc; page 6 © Michael Newman/PhotoEdit; pages 7, 17 (lower left)
© Getty Images; pages 8, 10-11, 14-15 Paul Dolan, pages 8-9 Laurence Parent;
page 12 © C.C. Lockwood/Earth Scenes; page 13 Dodie Ulery; page 16 Jim
Cummins/Getty Images; page 17 (lower right), 25 (lower) © Corbis; page 17
(top) © Hans-Bernard Huber/Getty Images; page 18 (middle right) © Michael
Habicht/Earth Scenes; pages 18-19 (lower) © Hanan Isachar/Corbis; page 19
(top-left) © W. Cody/Corbis; page 20 © Jim Wark/Airphoto; page 21 © Keren
Su/China Span; page 22 © Jay Dickman; page 23 © Jodi Cobb/National
Geographic Image Collection; page 24 © Catherine Karnow/Corbis;
page 25 (middle left) © Joseph Sohm/Corbis; page 26 © Corel; page 27
© Paul J. Hames/California Department of Water Resources;
pages 28, 29 Sharon Hoogstraten; page 31 © Kim Taylor/
Bruce Coleman Inc.

Produced through the worldwide resources of the National Geographic Society,
John M. Fahey, Jr., President and Chief Executive Officer; Gilbert M. Grosvenor,
Chairman of the Board; Nina D. Hoffman, Executive Vice President and
President, Books and Education Publishing Group.

PREPARED BY NATIONAL GEOGRAPHIC SCHOOL PUBLISHING
Ericka Markman, Senior Vice President and President, Children's Books and
Education Publishing Group, Steve Mico, Vice President, Editorial Director;
Rosemary Baker, Executive Editor; Barbara Seeber, Editorial Manager;
Jim Hiscott, Design Manager; Kristin Hanneman, Illustrations Manager;
Matt Wascavage, Manager of Publishing Services; Sean Philpotts, Production
Manager; Jane Ponton Production Artist.

Manufacturing and Quality Management
Christopher A. Liedel, Chief Financial Officer; Phillip L. Schlosser, Director;
Clifton M. Brown III, Manager.

PROGRAM DEVELOPER
Kate Boehm Jerome

ART DIRECTION
Daniel Banks, Project Design Company

CONSULTANT/REVIEWER
Dr. Timothy Cooney, Professor of Earth Science and Science Education,
University of Northern Iowa

BOOK DEVELOPMENT
Navta Associates

Published by the National Geographic Society
Washington, D.C. 20036-4688

Product No. 4J41766

ISBN: 0-7922-4572-5

Printed in Canada

11 10 09 08
10 9 8

Contents

Introduction 4
Old, Old Water

Chapter 1 6
Water in Motion:
Water, Water Everywhere

Picture This 14
Go With the Flow

Chapter 2 16
Uses of Water:
Water Works

Chapter 3 22
Future Water Supplies:
Water, Water . . . Where?

Thinking Like a Scientist 26
Interpreting Data

Hands-on Science 28
Pollution Solution

Science Notebook 30

Glossary 31

Index 32

Old, Old Water

Did you drink some of the same
water the dinosaurs splashed?

About 150 million years ago, the quiet waters of a shallow pond were broken by the splashing of an allosaur chasing dinner. About 500 years ago, a Native American family took shelter in their tepee during a thunderstorm. Half an hour ago, you might have taken a drink from your school's water fountain.

What do these events have in common? You, the family, and the dinosaurs all came in contact with Earth's limited supply of water. And here's the real surprise. You could be drinking some of the same water that rained on the tepee or splashed in the pond!

Water can travel. It can go from a river, to a lake, to a cloud, to rain. It can go from the juice in an orange, to the blood in your body, to pipes in a sewer system, and back into a river. But water doesn't disappear. And it doesn't make more of itself. So the water we have now is all we'll ever have.

How can we look after this water and make sure there's plenty for everyone? This book will show you the ins and outs of the world's water flow. It will show you how we can make clean, fresh water last far into the future.

Chapter 1

Water in Motion

Water, Water Everywhere

Even in the driest desert, there's water. It's in the air. It's below the ground. It's hanging from the thorns of a cactus as early morning dew.

Water in the air condenses onto cactus thorns.

Oceans cover nearly three-quarters of Earth's surface. That's why the planet looks blue from space.

You may not pay much attention to the water in your world. You notice it when you brush your teeth or take a shower. But there's much more that you can't see. It's hanging in the air. It's filling your body's cells and streaming through your veins. It's rushing through pipes all over town and lying deep beneath your feet.

All the World's Water

It may be hard to imagine the incredible amount of water on Earth. Start by looking at a globe. See all that blue? That represents about 200 billion liters of water for every man, woman, and child on the planet!

That doesn't mean that there's always plenty to drink, however. Most of Earth's water is salty ocean water. **Salt water** is fine for tuna, lobsters, and other sea creatures. But it's not fine for humans and most other animals.

Only 3 percent of Earth's water is **fresh water**. And most of that is locked up in **glaciers**. These giant ice blocks are found high on some mountains and near the North and South Poles. So where is the water we can use?

Look Underground

Thick layers of rock lie beneath the soil. Much of the rock has spaces like a sponge. The spaces can be as tiny as pinpoints or as big as caves. Water seeps down and collects in these spaces. Water can move along underground from space to space. This underground water storage area is called an **aquifer**.

An aquifer can be as small as a field or as large as a few states. The Ogallala Aquifer is the world's largest. It stretches from South Dakota to Texas.

Aquifer water is **groundwater**. The water flowing from your faucet may be groundwater. Five out of ten Americans drink it.

Do you think your drinking water comes from surface water or from groundwater?

Wells are dug to bring groundwater to the surface.
Sometimes a well pumps out all the water it can reach. A deeper well reaches more water.

Look On the Surface

Earth's **surface water** bodies are connected. Streams join and form larger rivers. Rivers run into lakes or oceans. Lakes and rivers spill over onto **wetlands,** which are soggy, swampy areas. Wetlands soak up water that could otherwise cause a flood.

Surface water is also connected to groundwater. Water in wetlands seeps down into the ground and refills aquifers.

Thinking Like a Scientist: Interpreting Data

When you need to compare lots of numbers, it helps to line them up in a chart. The chart below shows where Earth's water lies. If you want to find out how much groundwater there is, find the word "Groundwater." Then look to the right of that word to find the amount. How much is there?

Water source	Water volume in cubic miles
Oceans	317,000,000
Icecaps, Glaciers	7,000,000
Groundwater	2,000,000
Freshwater lakes	30,000
Inland seas	25,000
Soil moisture	16,000
Atmosphere	3,100
Rivers	300

Source: Nace, *The Hydrologic Cycle*, U.S. Geological Survey, 1984

Look at the chart. Where is most of Earth's water? Do freshwater lakes contain more water than rivers?

Streams and rivers flow downhill, like this stream in Pennsylvania.

The Water Cycle

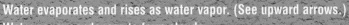

1 Water evaporates and rises as water vapor. (See upward arrows.)
2 Water vapor condenses to form clouds.
3 Water falls from clouds as rain or snow. (See downward arrows.)
4 Water returns to rivers, lakes, oceans, and aquifers, and the cycle begins again.

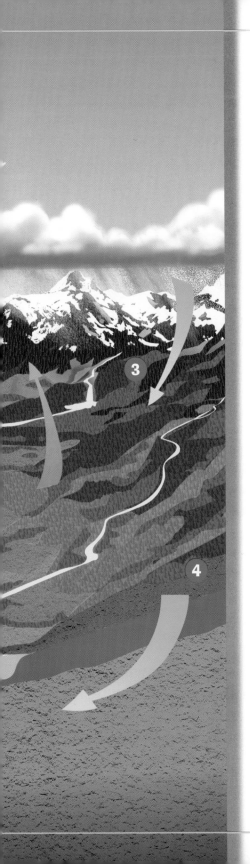

Water on the Go

Is it raining? Can you see clouds? If so, you're seeing part of the water cycle—the constant movement of water around the globe.

Water Rises Every day about 860 trillion liters (230 trillion gallons) of Earth's surface water **evaporates** into the air. The water becomes an invisible gas called **water vapor**. Plants also add water vapor to the air.

Water Condenses As water vapor drifts upward, it cools. As it cools, the vapor may **condense,** or turn back into water droplets. Or if the air is cold enough, the vapor forms tiny ice crystals. The droplets and crystals are smaller than the period at the end of this sentence. They gather to form clouds.

Water Falls When enough droplets or crystals cling together, they become heavy enough to fall. Depending on the weather, you might get rain, snow, or even hail.

Water Flows Some rainwater or melted snow trickles through the soil, watering plants or reaching an aquifer. Some runs downhill over the ground, forming streams that could end in a lake or an ocean. Little by little, this water turns to vapor and rises. The water cycle goes on and on.

Keeping It Clean

As water travels, it can run into some serious pollution. Although there are laws against it, some factories still spill out harmful chemicals. The chemicals might be piped into a river. Even chemicals dumped on the ground can seep into an aquifer. But that's not the only way people pollute water.

Farmers and gardeners spray their plants with fertilizers and **pesticides**. Rain washes these chemicals from plants and can carry them into ponds, rivers, lakes, or the ocean. Fertilizers that help plants grow can turn a pond into a green swamp, overgrown with water plants. Pesticides designed to kill bugs can hurt fish, frogs, and other animals.

Wastewater from factories may contain harmful chemicals.

People sometimes pollute without knowing it. Suppose you're fixing your bike chain in the driveway and spill a can of oil. If you don't clean it up right away, what happens? The next time it rains, water washes the oil down the driveway into the street gutter. Then it goes into the sewer. From there, it might go into a stream.

When water runs down a drain, it probably goes to a treatment plant. At the treatment plant, much of the pollution is taken out. But nasty chemicals like paint or turpentine might be too much for the treatment plant to handle.

Natural Cleanup

Dirty water can clean itself. When water evaporates, dirt stays behind. So when water vapor condenses and forms rain, the rain starts out clean. Then as raindrops fall to Earth, they mix with chemicals that float up from cars and factories. Some of these chemicals turn rain into acid rain. This type of pollution can kill trees and fish and can damage buildings. Laws have reduced acid rain but haven't stopped it.

Evaporation isn't nature's only way of cleaning water. On its way down to an aquifer, water is filtered clean by rock and soil. Wetland plants and **bacteria** can eat up some poisonous chemicals. The soil in wetlands breaks down some harmful chemicals. In fact, wetlands are so good at cleaning water that some factories create artificial wetlands to clean up their pollution!

Stay Tuned!

No Soap!

To help keep water clean, two scientists in Utah are working on a washing machine that doesn't need detergent. Detergent changes water so that it cleans better. This new machine would contain a solid material that does the same thing. Plus, it uses less water because there's no rinse cycle. Will it work? Stay tuned!

Wetlands help clean polluted water.

Picture This

Go With the Flow

Follow the numbers to see where your tap water comes from and where it goes.

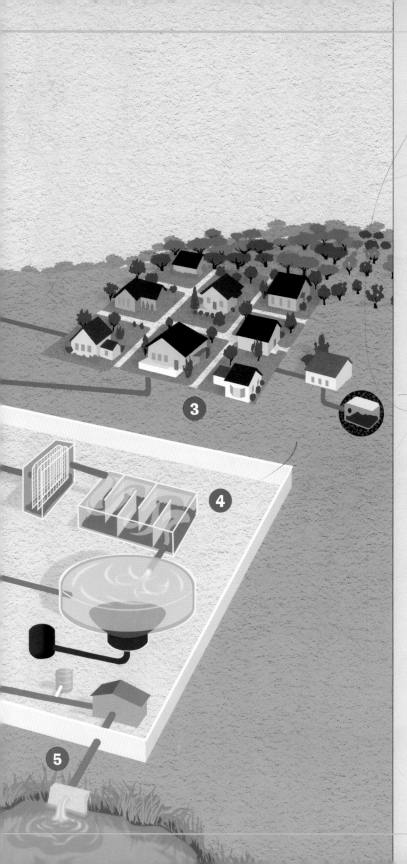

1 Water purification plant About half of the tap water in the United States gets pumped up from underground aquifers. (Some tap water comes from lakes and rivers, too.) Chemicals might be added to soften the water. A little chlorine is added to kill germs. (Water from lakes and rivers goes through other steps to remove fish, leaves, mud, and bacteria.)

2 Water tower Pumps lift water to a storage tower, usually on high ground.

3 Homes Gravity pulls water downhill through pipes into homes and other places. Used water swirls down the drain and runs through pipes into the sewer. (If you live far from a city, drained water might flow into an underground septic tank. Bacteria in the tank break down wastes. Cleaner water leaves the tank and goes into the ground.)

4 Sewage treatment plant The sewage is cleaned by using screens, filters, bacteria, and chlorine.

5 Lake It's clean! Now the water is safe to let out into a river or lake.

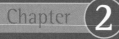

Chapter 2

Uses of Water

Water Works

Water may be a lot of fun, but it also does a lot of work. It nourishes plants, makes electrical power, quenches people's thirst, washes clothes, and more.

If you're an average American, you use about 380 liters (about 100 gallons) of water a day! That's enough to fill 2½ bathtubs. Sound like too much? Well, think about all the ways you and your family use water. Drinking. Washing. Brushing. Flushing. Showering. Bathing. Sprinkling. You get the idea. It all adds up to a lot of water.

Water for drinking

But it's nothing compared to farms and factories. Around the world, farms soak up nearly two-thirds of the water used each day. Industry uses a surprising amount of water, too. It takes 50 liters (13 gallons) to make the plastic in one action figure. It takes about 800 liters (200 gallons) to make a pair of jeans.

More People, More Water

Earth's population is growing—fast. In the past 100 years, it has increased from about 2 billion to over 6 billion. As more people put more demands on the same amount of water, trouble starts. Using water for one purpose takes it away from another purpose. You'll see how on the next few pages.

Water for fighting fires

Water to make electricity

Getting Water to Plants

Irrigation, or the movement of water to crops, has been around for at least 5,000 years. Ancient Egyptians were the first to dig ditches that directed river water to crops. Thanks to irrigation, Egyptians could plant more than one crop a year. As a result, there was plenty of food for a large population. Their cities grew.

Today about 40 percent of crops worldwide are irrigated. Farmers often irrigate by pumping water through large sprinklers. A few farmers have switched to water-saving drip irrigation. Hoses with holes drop water directly onto plant roots. So less water evaporates.

Getting Water to People

Throughout history, **aqueducts** have carried water from rivers or lakes to cities. In ancient Rome, water flowed through tunnels and over bridges to supply a thirsty Roman Empire.

Today tunnel systems carry water to major cities. Hot, dry southern California depends on a large system of dams, pipes, and pumps. Water from the Colorado River is redirected over mountains to quench California's thirst.

Modern aqueducts pipe water over long distances.

Ancient Roman aqueduct in Israel

Water wheels powered machines that ground corn, cut lumber, spun cotton, and did many other jobs.

Doing Heavy Work

The year is 1607. English settlers sail across the Atlantic Ocean to the New World. They build houses on the James River in Virginia. They grow vegetables and hunt animals. The settlers wait for another English ship to deliver flour so they can bake bread—if the mice don't eat it on the long journey.

Fast forward to 1621. The settlers of Jamestown build their first mill to grind corn into flour. Finally, fresh flour for bread!

Without the mill, Jamestown may not have survived. What made the mill work? Flowing water from the James River. Water pushed against the paddles of a large water wheel. The wheel turned. That turning spun a heavy round stone inside the mill. The stone ground corn or grain into powder. That's flour!

Hoover Dam provides electricity and water when it is needed.

From Water Wheels to Electricity

Here's a simple recipe for electricity. Take an old water wheel. Update it to make it more efficient. Then hook it to a machine called a generator. Presto! The power of moving water turns into **hydroelectricity**. One of every 14 Americans gets electricity from water.

To make hydroelectricity, you need lots of fast-moving water. If the water is falling, or can be made to fall, all the better. Where do you think are the most likely places to have a hydroelectric plant? You guessed it—waterfalls and dams.

Dams: Wonders and Woes

Hoover Dam was hailed as an engineering Wonder of the World when it was completed in 1935. Before they could build, workers had to move the Colorado River out of the way. They blasted giant tunnels in the rock around the river. River water flowed through the tunnels, away from the dam site.

Thousands of men poured more than six million tons of concrete to build the dam. When the river flowed back into place, it smacked against the concrete. The water rose high to form a huge **reservoir** called Lake Mead.

Open a pipe in the dam and water from Lake Mead floods through, turning high-tech water wheels. That power turns a generator and becomes electricity—for 1.3 million people. Lake Mead provides water when people need it for farms, homes, and industry. It is also a nice place for fishing and boating.

Although dams solve some problems, they can create others. The land behind the dam—whether farmland, forest, or even towns—is flooded by the reservoir. In India, dams have pushed 38 million people from their homes. A huge dam being built in China will flood some of that country's best farmland.

Downstream from dams, fish and other wildlife may get just a trickle when the gates are closed and a flood when they're open. These changes reduce wildlife in the area.

Dams are still being built. But people around the world are looking for other ways of getting fresh water.

A dam being built in China forces people to move to higher ground.

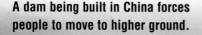

Did you ever

wonder...

...how many dams there are?

Worldwide, there are about 40,000 dams that are taller than a four-story building, and 800,000 smaller ones.

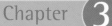

Future Water Supplies

Water, Water . . . Where?

Water levels in the Great Lakes have been falling in recent years. Can you tell where the water used to be?

D o you worry about having enough water to drink? Hot, dry countries such as Egypt and Israel have to worry about water all the time. In the record-hot summer of 2002, much of the United States worried, too. Reservoir levels fell. **Drought** spread to 36 of the 50 states.

Cities looked for ways to **conserve,** or save, water. Many **rationed** water. Outdoor watering was allowed only on certain days of the week. Other communities banned outdoor watering altogether. These solutions have been used in the past. But some people are coming up with innovative ways to increase water supplies.

De-Salt It

Santa Barbara, on the California coast, is always dry. But in the 1990s it got stuck in a long, serious drought. So the city decided to build one of the nation's first **desalination** plants. These factories take the salt out of seawater. This allowed the city to change salt water into fresh water.

Over the years, scientists have worked to make desalination methods cheaper and easier. Still, desalination plants are expensive. And they eat up huge amounts of energy. Experts recommend it in a pinch, when other solutions fail.

Water levels in Lake Huron have dropped more than a meter (3 feet) in recent years.

Save It

Most of southern California fought a long drought by saving water. By 1993, people used only about half the water they had used in 1990. Those levels have stayed fairly low since.

How do they do it? They start by thinking about what they need and what they don't need. For example, people decided that thick, green lawns are nice, but not as important as having water to drink. So towns set strict limits on watering lawns. Water police give tickets to rule breakers. Some people have replaced lawns with plants that need little water.

Water companies pay people to switch to water-saving toilets and washing machines. People take quick showers. They hang up their towels to dry instead of throwing them in the wash. They don't let the water run while brushing their teeth. These simple actions save billions of gallons every year.

This garden in Montecito, California, contains native plants that need little water.

Reuse It, Recycle It

As you read this, billions of gallons of water are swirling down drains and rushing out of pipelines. Most of this water will be cleaned and released in a river or lake. Nearly 100 years ago, people in California asked: Why not use this water again *before* we let it go? California began to send treated wastewater to farms, factories, and golf courses. Today this recycled water is also piped onto land where it can trickle down into aquifers.

Many cities have begun to recycle water. Individuals recycle water, too. Some people take showers with buckets on the floor. You wouldn't want to drink the water that collects. But it's perfectly fine for watering plants.

If you think about it, recycling water is not such a strange idea. Remember, Earth's water has been recycled by nature for billions of years. So the next time you turn on your faucet, remember that the water coming out has a long history. With everyone pitching in, it will have a long, clean future, too.

WE'RE SAVING WATER TOO!

CITY OF SANTA CLARA
1777 THE 1852
MISSION CITY

WATER CONSERVATION AREA

Many cities are conserving water. How can you help?

Interpreting Data

Scientists work with a lot of information, or data. Scientists often arrange data into graphs in order to tell what all the information means.

One kind of graph is made of bars that represent certain amounts. The bar graph on the next page shows how much water people use for different jobs every day. The left edge of the graph has a scale that shows number of liters. To find out how much water people use for a bath, find the bar labeled "Bath." Put your finger on the top of that bar. Then trace a straight line over to the left edge. You can see that a typical bath uses 150 liters (about 39 gallons) of water.

Practice the Skill

Use the bar graph to answer these questions.

1. Which job uses the most water?

2. Which job uses the least water?

3. How much more water is used to take a bath than a shower?

4. About how much water is used to brush your teeth with the water running?

5. From looking at the graph, what are some good ways to save water?

Check It Out

Sprinkling the lawn might use 1,900 liters (about 502 gallons) of water. How would you have to change the graph to add that information to it?

Water for Everyday Jobs

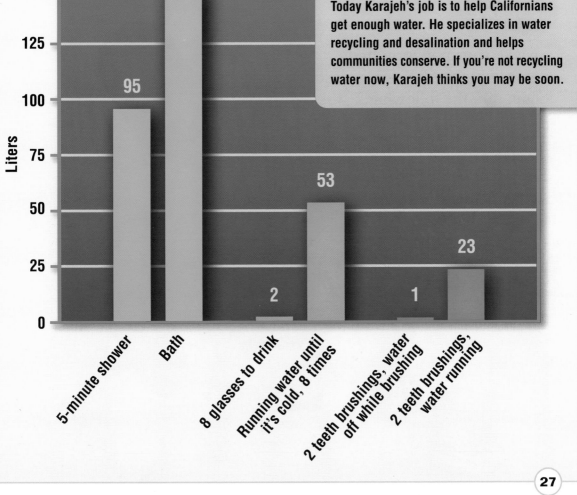

Fawzi Karajeh (FOW-zi Kah-rah-JEH): Water and Soil Scientist

Fawzi Karajeh grew up in the Middle East, where fresh water is scarce. The only source of drinking water for Karajeh and his family was rain collected in shallow wells. Karajeh learned that every drop of water counts. Today Karajeh's job is to help Californians get enough water. He specializes in water recycling and desalination and helps communities conserve. If you're not recycling water now, Karajeh thinks you may be soon.

Pollution Solution

There are many different ways to clean up pollution. Some are better for certain types of pollution. Some are just easier, faster, or cheaper than other methods. Try out two methods on your own "pollution brew" and see how they compare.

Materials
✓ 2 paper coffee filters
✓ 2 rubber bands
✓ Small square of plastic wrap
✓ Measuring cup
✓ Measuring spoon
✓ Baking soda
✓ White vinegar
✓ Ketchup
✓ Black pepper
✓ Cooking oil
✓ 3 clear plastic cups
✓ Marker
✓ Plastic spoon

SAFETY TIP: When working with liquids, wipe up any spills immediately.

Explore

1   Make your pollution brew. *(See photograph A.)* In a plastic cup, mix the following:

    1 cup of water
    1/2 tsp of black pepper
    1/2 tsp of baking soda
    1 tsp of cooking oil
    2 tsp of ketchup

A

2 Use the marker to label two other plastic cups A and B. Each cup will stand for a different method of cleaning the brew.

3 Stir the pollution brew. Then pour half of it into cup A. Cover the cup with plastic wrap and hold it in place with a rubber band. Place the cup on a sunny windowsill.

4 Put two coffee filters together. Put them into cup B so that the filters fold over the edge. Hold them in place with a rubber band.

5 Pour the rest of the pollution brew into the coffee filters. Wait about 5 minutes for it to drain. *(See photograph B.)*

6 Observe what pollution the coffee filters caught. What pollution went through the filters? Can you tell if the baking soda went through?

7 Remove the filters and test for baking soda by adding about $1/2$ tsp of vinegar to the filtered mixture. If it bubbles or fizzes, the baking soda is still there.

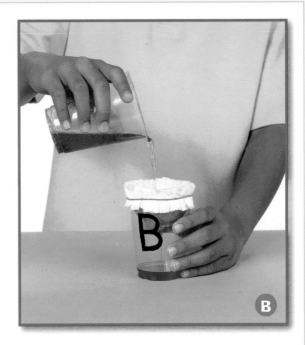

8 After a few hours, check cup A on the windowsill. Remove it when there are drops of water on the plastic. Observe the drops. Can you see any pollution? Look closely. Take off the plastic wrap and turn it over. Then test by sprinkling a few drops of vinegar on the water. Put your ear close. Can you hear fizzing?

Think

Which method filtered more water? Which method was slower, but cleaned more kinds of pollution out of the water?

Science Notebook

WATER WONDERS

- Every living thing is made of at least some water. About 60 percent of the human body is water.

- It takes about 15 million cloud droplets to make one raindrop.

- Water is more dense as a liquid than as a solid. That's why ice floats.

- Pure water has no color. It reflects the colors that surround it. Under a blue sky, water looks blue.

- A mouthful of ocean water can be as salty as a mouthful of potato chips. Much of the ocean's salt comes from rocks on the ocean floor. Some salt is carried to the ocean by rivers.

WEBSITES TO VISIT

Environmental Explorers' Club
Fun information about different water ecosystems.
http://www.epa.gov/kids/water.htm

U.S. Environmental Protection Agency
Interesting sites filled with facts, games, and activities about water.
http://www.epa.gov/OW/kids.html
http://www.epa.gov/safewater/kids/games.html

U.S. Geological Survey's Water Science for Schools
Fascinating facts and fun activities about water.
http://ga.water.usgs.gov/edu/

BOOKS TO READ

Hooper, Meredith. *The Drop in My Drink: The Story of Water on Our Planet*. Viking Children's Book, 1998.

Locker, Thomas. *Water Dance*. Voyager Books, 2002.

MacQuitty, Miranda. *Eyewitness: Ocean*. Dorling Kindersley, 2000.

Parker, Steve and Philip Dowell. *Eyewitness: Pond & River*. Dorling Kindersley, 2000.

Glossary

aqueduct – an artificial channel for carrying water. It can be above ground or below ground.

aquifer – a buried layer of rock, sand, or gravel that holds water

bacteria – microscopic creatures, made of one cell only, that are found inside us and all around us

condense – to go from a gas to a liquid

conserve – to save or not waste

desalination – the process of taking the salt out of salt water to make it fresh water

drought – a long period of dryness, enough to damage or kill plants

evaporate – to go from a liquid to a gas

fresh water – Earth's water that's not salty, such as lakes, rivers, and groundwater. We drink fresh water.

glacier – a huge mass of ice that slowly slides, or spreads out, over land

groundwater – water buried underground in an aquifer

hydroelectricity – electricity produced from water power

irrigation – the movement of water to plants by artificial methods such as sprinklers or human-made canals

pesticides – chemicals designed to kill insects or other animals that eat plants

ration – to allow only certain amounts to be used

reservoir – a lake created to store water

salt water – water that contains large amounts of natural salts. Ocean water is salt water.

surface water – rivers, streams, lakes, ponds, wetlands, oceans or any other body of water that lies on Earth's surface

water vapor – water that has turned to gas

wetland – land such as marshes and swamps that are wet at least part of the year

Index

acid rain 13

aqueducts 18

aquifer 8, 11–13, 15

bacteria 13

bar graph 26–27

condense 11

conserve 23

dams 20–21

desalination 23, 27

drought 23–24

evaporates 11, 13

fresh water 7, 21, 23

glaciers 7

groundwater 8–9

hydroelectricity 20

irrigation 18

Karajeh, Fawzi 27

mill 19

pesticides 12

pollution 12–13

ration 23

recycled water 25, 27

reservoir 21, 23

salt water 7, 23

sewage treatment plant 15

surface water 9

water cycle 10–11

water vapor 11

water wheel 19–21

wetlands 9, 13